SUPER CITIES!

PORTLAND

by Cindy Collins-Taylor

arcadia®
CHILDREN'S BOOKS

Published by Arcadia Children's Books
A Division of Arcadia Publishing
Charleston, SC
www.arcadiapublishing.com

Super Cities is a trademark of Arcadia Publishing, Inc.

First published 2021

Manufactured in the United States

ISBN 978-1-4671-9853-0

Library of Congress Control Number: 2021943258

Produced by Shoreline Publishing Group LLC
Santa Barbara, California
Designer: Patty Kelley

Contents

Portland!

FAST FACTS
Portland, Oregon

POPULATION:
665,000

FOUNDED:
1851

AREA:
145 square miles

Portland, Oregon

ATTENTION READERS!

This book is NOT about Portland, Maine. Thank you. (But stay tuned!)

Look at a map of the west (left) side of the United States. See those three big states that touch the Pacific Ocean? The one in the middle is Oregon. At the very top, you'll find Oregon's biggest city. That's Portland!

Portland is filled with fun things to see and do. Take a tram *waaay* up a very steep hill, and see Portland spread out before you. Put your nose into ten thousand roses and sniff away! Enter a huge store the size of an entire city block . . . it's stuffed to the ceiling with books and more books.

If you like being out in nature but also like busy streets and tall buildings, then you'll like Portland. It's a bustling city that has many forests, hills, parks, and places to be on, in, or near water. You'll notice lots of bridges. They help people cross Portland's two big rivers.

The city is known for its beauty—and for its unusual personality. People there like to do things in their own ways. Portlanders think: *Why not be different?*

Inside this book, we'll find out more about this amazing place and meet some of the people who have helped make the city so special. **Let's go to Portland!**

PORTLAND: Map It!

Portland is nicknamed River City because it was built at a place where two rivers join. The great Willamette River flows north and meets the mighty Columbia River rolling in from the east.

In Portland, you'll see giant cargo ships moving slowly up and down the Columbia River to and from the Pacific Ocean. They move everything from apples to zippers in and out of the city. On the Willamette River, people like to fish and kayak or relax on ferry boat cruises. You could even take a thrilling ride on a high-speed jetboat. But bring a towel—you'll probably get soaked!

The Willamette River divides the east side from the west side of the city. Portland has five major parts: North, Northwest, Southwest, Northeast, and Southeast. Each region has its own personality and types of neighborhoods.

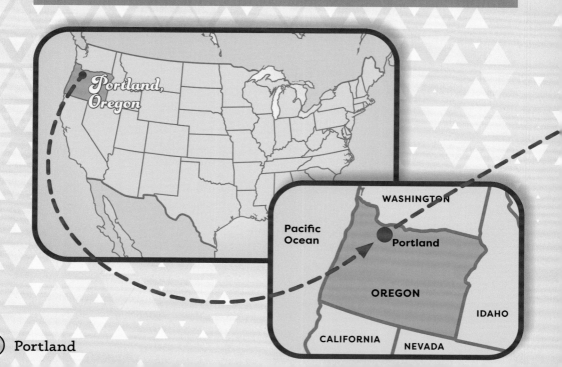

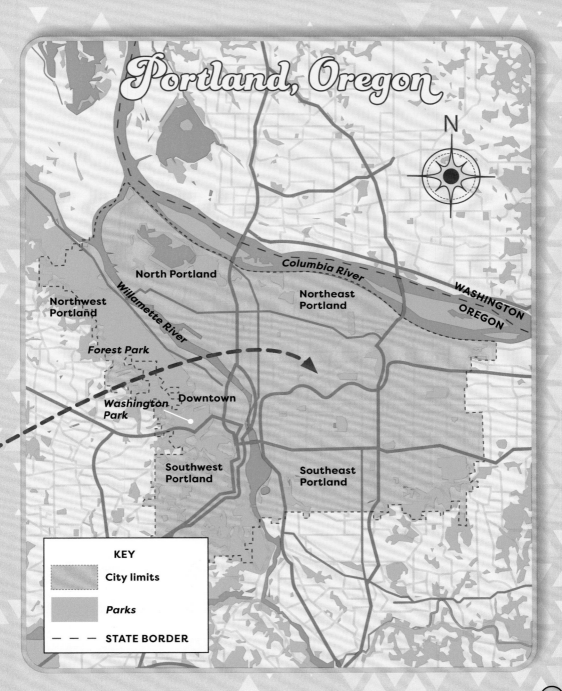

Portland, Oregon

North Portland

Northwest Portland

Northeast Portland

Willamette River

Columbia River

WASHINGTON
OREGON

Forest Park

Washington Park

Downtown

Southwest Portland

Southeast Portland

N

KEY

City limits

Parks

– – – STATE BORDER

Bridges!
We Got Bridges!

Getting around in Bridgetown often means using bridges. (That checks out!) Here are the city's 15 spans and the years they were built.

ACROSS THE COLUMBIA

To the north of downtown, the Columbia River flows mightily. These are the key local bridges over that famous waterway:

Burlington Northern Railroad Bridge (1908)
Interstate Bridge (1917)
Glenn L. Jackson Memorial Bridge (1982)

ACROSS THE WILLAMETTE

Here are the bridges that cross the Willamette River, shown with the year they opened to traffic:

Burlington Northern Railroad Bridge (1908)
Hawthorne Bridge (1910)
Steel Bridge (1912)
Broadway Bridge (1913)
Ross Island Bridge (1922)
Sellwood Bridge (1925)
Burnside Bridge (1926)
St. Johns Bridge (1931)
Morrison Bridge (1958)
Marquam (I-5) Bridge (1966)
Fremont Bridge (1973)
Tilikum Crossing (2015)

NAMED BY A COIN FLIP!

The area we know as Portland, Oregon, is located on the traditional lands of native peoples, including the Chinook, Multnomah, and, Clackamas. They had their own languages and names for everything in the region, of course.

By 1845, white pioneers Asa Lovejoy of Boston, Massachusetts, and Francis Pettygrove of Portland, Maine, had moved to the area and built a town. All that building (with wood) left the remains of trees all over the place. People started calling the area "Stumptown."

Lovejoy and Pettygrove decided to pick something better to call it. But there was a problem. Each man wanted to name it after his own home city. They agreed that a coin flip was a fair way to choose. So, they tossed a copper penny in the air. Pettygrove (and Portland) won.

Amazingly, that famous "Portland Penny" is still around. You can see it downtown at the Oregon Historical Society.

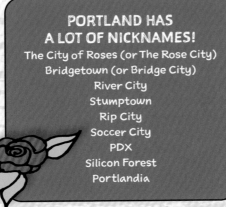

Francis Pettygrove

Asa Lovejoy

PORTLAND HAS A LOT OF NICKNAMES!
The City of Roses (or The Rose City)
Bridgetown (or Bridge City)
River City
Stumptown
Rip City
Soccer City
PDX
Silicon Forest
Portlandia

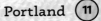

THE CITY OF
Roses

Portland is called the City of Roses for a good reason. In 1888, a type of large, pink, French rose was introduced to Portland. Turns out, roses grow very well in the mild-but-damp Northwest climate. Portlanders went nuts for the thorny beauties and planted them everywhere. By 1905, sweet-smelling bushes lined 20 miles of city streets!

Two years later, in 1907, Portland held its first Rose Festival. The annual event has been going strong ever since. Each June, people celebrate their favorite city and flower with a waterfront carnival, the crowning of a Rose Queen, and marching band music. For the festival highlight—the Rose Parade—Portlanders make floats covered in, you guessed it . . . roses!

FAST FACTS

At the International Rose Test Garden:
* 10,000 individual rose bushes
* 650 varieties
* About 700,000 visitors annually
* 4.5 acres
* Blooming season runs from April through October.
* Peak bloom usually happens in June—in time for the Rose Festival!
* Rose breeders from many countries donate about 2,500 rose bushes to the garden per year.

A Rosy View

More than 100 years ago, Portland's nursery owners began planting lots and lots of rose bushes in Washington Park. They wanted to make sure that the many kinds of roses found in Europe survived World War I.

In 1917, the site was officially named "The International Rose Test Garden." When it later opened to the public, it was a big hit . . . and still is! Hundreds of thousands of people wander through the garden every year, trying to choose their favorite rose.

FAST FACT

The garden grows roses named for all former Prime Ministers of the Royal Rosarians, a group of goodwill ambassadors. These friendly folks meet people from all over the world and introduce them to Portland. Rosarians are easy to spot in their all-white suits with red roses on the sleeves.

HISTORY: Early Days

For thousands of years before the famous 1845 coin toss, people lived in villages along the Columbia and Willamette rivers, in the area we now know as Portland. Many belonged to the Chinook Nation, a group of Northwest tribes.

In 1805, members of the famous Lewis and Clark expedition passed through the area. They continued to the west of what is now Portland until they finally saw the great Pacific. Clark caught the moment in his journal: "Ocean in View!"

Save it for later! Native peoples caught lots of salmon and dried the leftovers. These preserved fish were safe to eat for many months, which got them through the winters.

Native peoples took things from nature to make what they needed. For example, they wore coats made of pounded cedar tree bark to stay warm and dry.

Some Native peoples believed birds and animals represented their guardian spirits. Archaeologists have found carvings and other art of those spirits made long ago.

HISTORY: Early Days

1811: The Oregon Trail began, made by fur traders and trappers. The trail started in Independence, Missouri, and stretched more than 2,000 miles, all the way to the Willamette Valley, near Portland. For decades, white settlers used it to travel west: on foot, on horseback, and by wagon.

1824: Dr. John McLoughlin arrived in the region. He was a bigshot in the Hudson's Bay Co., a powerful Canadian fur-trading business. McLoughlin helped develop Fort Vancouver, just over the Columbia River from what became Portland. That helped speed up white settlement in the area. McLoughlin has been called "The Father of Oregon."

1850: By the mid-1800s, the white people that had taken over the region often treated the Indigenous people very badly. In 1850, the government passed a law that stole land away from the Native people and gave it to white settlers—for free! Unjustly, many of the Native Americans whose families had lived in the area for generations were forced to move inland, to reservations.

1851: In the year that the City of Portland officially began, its first public school opened. The teacher was John T. Outhouse. Yes, that was really his name!

1860: Full steam ahead! The Oregon Steam Navigation Company brought steamboats to Portland and helped make the area an important freight port.

1868: A company started building rail lines on the east side of the Willamette River. The very next day, a competing company began construction of another railway— on the west side! That was the start of Portland's first long-distance railroads.

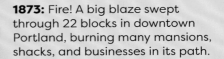

1873: Fire! A big blaze swept through 22 blocks in downtown Portland, burning many mansions, shacks, and businesses in its path.

1896: Portland's grand Union Station opened. You can still ride trains in and out of this beautiful depot!

1905: Portland held the Lewis and Clark Centennial Exposition to mark the 100th anniversary of their famous 1804-06 journey. The huge event ran for four months. About 1.6 million people from all over the world came to the city to see fascinating exhibits from 26 countries.

1917: The Interstate Bridge was completed. For the first time, traffic could cross back and forth over the Columbia River between Washington State and Oregon.

1941: The Portland Columbia Airport opened next to the river it was named for. Today it's known as Portland International Airport, or PDX.

1948: Vanport was a town just outside north Portland, near the Columbia River. It was built by the US government to house shipyard workers, many of them African American. On May 30, a nearby dike (small dam) collapsed. A ten-foot wall of water rushed to Vanport, and destroyed the town. Fifteen people were killed and about 18,000 people lost their homes! Vanport was wiped off the map forever.

1962: A ferocious storm hit Portland and the Pacific Northwest on October 12. The wind, rain, and mudslides from the "Columbus Day Storm" did major damage to buildings, roads, cars, trees, power lines—you name it. Portland saw wind gusts up to 116 miles per hour. At least 46 people died.

1980: Mount St. Helens blew its top! After weeks of rumblings, the famous volcano in southern Washington state erupted—big time—on the morning of May 18. Hundreds of square miles of forests became smoking wastelands, and 57 people were killed. In Portland, more than 50 miles to the south, ash from the explosion piled high on streets, roofs, and cars. When the air cleared, you could see that part of the peak had been blown off. The mountain had a new, flatter shape!

People from the Past!

Portland's history is filled with interesting and amazing people. Here are a few to know about.

Abigail Scott Duniway (1834-1915)

In 1852, when she was 17, Duniway's family traveled the Oregon Trail from Illinois to Portland—in a wagon pulled by on ox. Abigail became a writer and an editor of a Portland newspaper that published articles in favor of women's rights—especially the very important right to vote!

FAST FACT

Famous Portland artist Mark Rothko helped popularize the modern abstract painting style. He expressed himself with colors and shapes instead of recognizable objects.

McCants Stewart (1877-1919)

After studying under Booker T. Washington at the famous Tuskegee Institute, Stewart became Oregon's first Black attorney. He became a leader for civil rights, fighting cases of discrimination.

Linus Pauling (1901–1994)

One of the greatest scientists of all time, Pauling was a chemist, biochemist, chemical engineer, author, educator, and peace activist. Pauling published more than 1,200 papers and books. That's one busy guy! In 1954, he received science's top award: The Nobel Prize for Chemistry.

James Beard (1903–1985)

Beard was an accomplished chef, educator, cookbook writer, and television personality. He helped popularize TV cooking shows and the use of fresh, in-season ingredients in American dishes. Today, the best chefs and restaurant professionals dream about winning a famous award that bears his name.

FAST FACT

Hacky Sack, a sport that involves kicking around a little bean bag to keep it in the air, was invented in the Portland area in 1972. It's still going strong!

Portland has never been quite as famous as its northern neighbor, Seattle, Washington. In recent years, though, the City of Roses has definitely become better known! Here are some of the things people think about when they think about Portland.

Bridges: They don't call it "Bridgetown" for nothing! Twelve span the Willamette, and three cross the wide Columbia.

Biking: Do you like to ride bikes? Yes? Well, Portlanders do too! The city has tens of thousands of enthusiastic cyclists and 162 miles of bike lanes. On some streets, two-wheelers outnumber cars by a huge margin!

Soccer: One of Portland's many nicknames is "Soccer City." (By the way, how did one place get so many nicknames?) The "beautiful game" has been hugely popular there for many decades.

Saving the Countryside: Portlanders care deeply about helping the environment. In 1979, voters said "yes please!" to the Urban Growth Boundary. It's an imaginary line around the highly populated area that helps protect farms, fields, and forests on the other side.

PORTLAND for Everyone

Old Town/Chinatown

If you walk through Portland's Old Town, you'll come across a colorful and beautifully carved gate with a pair of lions standing guard. It was put up in 1986 to mark the entrance to the Chinatown part of the district.

Chinese people have lived in Portland since the 1850s. That's when the California Gold Rush attracted many looking to find jobs in gold mining, fishing, and railroad building. People from Asian countries besides China emigrated as well. In fact, up until World War II, Portland's Chinatown

was more commonly called "Japantown." Asian Portlandians have contributed richly to the city over the decades, even while facing terrible discrimination and racism throughout history.

Portland's Black History and Culture

More than 200 years ago, African Americans were among some of the earliest non-native people to settle in Oregon. But their population in the state remained small until World War II, when tens of thousands of Black workers came to Portland and other places in the Northwest for jobs in the shipyards and railroads. Traditionally, African Americans lived in Portland's inner North and Northeast sections due to racist laws prohibiting them from buying land or homes in other areas. Despite being segregated and excluded in many areas of growth (until the 1970s), Black Portlanders had a huge influence on the culture of the area.

Prominent Black Portlanders include: Charles Jordan, the first African-American city commissioner and director of Portland Parks & Recreation, who was also a noted environmentalist; jazz musicians Esperanza Spalding, Mel Brown, and Janice Scroggins; early civil rights activist and newspaper publisher Beatrice Morrow Cannady; and former NBA All-Star and businessman Terrell Brandon.

Indigenous People in Portland

Humans first came to the Columbia and Willamette river basin about 11,000 years ago. Even though they were forced off their land by the government, the descendants of more than 380 tribes continue to live in and near Portland. The community often holds cultural events like powwows and celebrations of salmon, the fish that's long been a major part of Native Americans' diets and traditions.

Nordic Influence

In the 1800s and early 1900s, tens of thousands of Scandinavian people came to the Pacific Northwest from the countries of Denmark, Finland, Iceland, Norway, and Sweden. They found jobs in industries familiar to them—like timber, fishing, and boatbuilding. The Nordic people had a big influence on the growth and culture of Portland. Today the home base for all things Scandinavian is Portland's Nordic Northwest building.

Portland's Latinx People

Spanish explorers and Mexican *vaqueros* (cowboys) were some of the first Spanish-speaking people to arrive in the Pacific Northwest. In World War II, many people from Mexico moved to Portland to work in the shipyards and fill other jobs left vacant by the war. In the decades that followed, many people from Mexico and Central and South America moved to the area in search of work and better lives. Today Latinx people are Oregon's largest ethnic group. Noted members of the community include: Cipriano Ferrel, a farmworker advocate and union founder; Kaleb Canales, the first Mexican-American coach in NBA history; saxophone player and band leader Gabriel Martinez; and José Eduardo González and Dañel Malan, who created Portland's Milagro-Miracle Theatre Group.

Rose City Russians

In recent years, thousands of people from former Soviet Union countries have moved to Portland. The area is home to more than 50,000 Russian and Ukrainian immigrants, and Russian is now the third most common language spoken in Oregon (after English and Spanish).

Rain? Can't Complain!
Portland Climate and Weather

In Portland, water often falls from the sky. Some sort of drizzle or drenching happens almost—but not quite—half the days in the year. Not everyone minds, though. Many Portlanders think: *Well, we want to be clean and green . . . so bring on the rain!*

A River . . . of Air

You already know that Portland has two major rivers on the ground. But did you know that it has a third river—in the sky? That's the jet stream (red stuff at right), a fast-traveling river of air that zips around the earth—often directly above the Pacific Northwest. On its journey, it picks up water vapor rising from the Pacific Ocean.

Blocked by Mountains

Some of the moisture gets trapped when it runs into the Cascade Mountains. The "stuck" mist gathers into clouds. The vapor forms droplets that fall onto Portland as rain.

Rising Air Cools and Condenses

Dry Air Advances

Warm Moist Air

Prevailing Winds

Rain Shadow

It's Snowing! Hooray!

It doesn't snow every winter in Portland, but every few years or so, jet stream moisture plus very cold temperatures make the snow come down hard! Schools and many businesses shut down, sometimes for days. Portlanders sled, create snow people and snow animals, wage fierce snowball fights with strangers, and even cross the city on skis to meet up with friends or pick up some hot cocoa.

Long Days

During Portland summers, the daylight really sticks around. That's because the city is located fairly far north. If you're in town on the Fourth of July, you'll have to wait until after 10 p.m. to watch fireworks displays. That's when the sky finally gets dark enough to make a good backdrop for the colorful explosions!

When to Visit

If you visit Portland in July, August, or September, you might ask: *Where the heck is all that rain I've heard about?* That's because those months are the dry ones. If you come in the winter when it's cool and rainy, just do what the Portlanders do: wear layers, and use a good raincoat!

Things to see in Portland

Tourist time! If you're from Portland, you (probably) know all about these places. But if you're visiting, here are some of the awesome places you can drag your parents to!

Pioneer Courthouse Square

Portlanders like to find nice outdoor spots to watch people and dogs go by as they sip their coffee. (And, oh boy, do Portlanders love their coffee!) One of the best places to do that is Pioneer Courthouse Square (at left). It's called "Portland's living room" because it's such a great place to hang out. But the red-brick square is not just for lounging. More than 300 events are held there each year, including concerts, political rallies, cultural festivals, and an annual holiday tree lighting. So, stop by the square if you're in town. There's sure to be something interesting going on!

Powell's City of Books

With nine huge rooms chock full of new and used books divided into 3,500 sections, Powell's is a great place to spend a morning . . . or an afternoon . . . or maybe an entire day.

Old Town/ Chinatown

There's a ton of things to do in this section of downtown Portland.

Saturday Market: On the weekends, the area closes its streets to cars and opens them to shoppers and browsers who come to its Saturday Market. This huge outdoor arts and crafts fair began in 1974—which makes it the oldest continually operating market of its kind in the United States. Local artists sell their works while musicians play for crowds and vendors dish up many kinds of food.

Keep on Bubbling! What are those basins of bubbling water? Businessman Simon Benson wanted to help his city, so he donated money to the city in 1912. Soon, dozens of bronze drinking fountains appeared around Old Town and the greater downtown area. These beloved "Benson Bubblers" have been running ever since, offering a steady stream of fresh drinking water to thirsty Portlanders and tourists alike.

Voodoo Doughnut: The wacky flavors, toppings, shapes, and names of Voodoo Doughnuts have made the shop a popular snack stop for many years. At PDX (the airport), you might even spot travelers carrying its familiar pink boxes back to far-flung destinations.

Lan Su Chinese Garden: This peaceful oasis in the middle of the city features beautifully carved stonework and plants native to China. Visit the tea house to enjoy a warm drink and soak up the beauty.

Underground Portland Tour

Go below Old Town to see the gritty underside of the city. Walk through eerie tunnels and find out about some of the shadier parts of Portland's past—like kidnapping, and illegally selling people to sea captains who wanted sailors! Some people believe kidnapped sailors still haunt these tunnels.

Things to see in Portland

Sauvie Island

When you're on this island, you're out in the country—but also within city limits. It's a great place to hike, bike, and birdwatch in any season. Look for long-legged cranes and herons, as well as majestic bald eagles. In the summer, harvest your own berries, peaches, and flowers, relax on a sandy Columbia River beach, or attend an outdoor concert. In the fall, pick apples or pumpkins, pet some friendly farm animals, go for a hayride. If you get your courage up, enter the "haunted" corn maze!

Crystal Springs Rhododendron Garden

Roses aren't the only beloved flower in Portland. The city also adores its rhododendrons! Visit in late April through June to see colorful blossoms galore.

Cool Places to Shop and Stroll

Both Portlanders and tourists like to visit bustling neighborhood districts to browse in trendy shops and grab a bite (or more) to eat. Here are some great places to do that:

SE Hawthorne: Hawthorne Boulevard is a very walkable street with blocks of vintage shops, quirky stores, and cafés and restaurants.

Nob Hill: San Francisco has a famous Nob Hill—so does Portland! Enjoy the fun boutiques and delicious treats that await you on NW 21st and NW 23rd Streets. Try Salt & Straw ice cream. Its flavors are *very* creative!

Alberta Street: The area between NE 15th and NE 25th avenues offers lots of stylish clothing stores, thrift shops, and art galleries.

The Pearl District: Once a gritty industrial zone, "The Pearl" is now an inviting place to walk around and pop into chic stores and eateries.

Oaks Amusement Park

Who doesn't like to soar to the top of a giant Ferris wheel, get dizzy on a Tilt-A-Whirl, or scream their lungs out on a roller coaster? Go to Oaks Amusement Park and you'll find these rides and many others—plus a mini golf course and a grand old roller-skating rink.

Make a SPLASH in Fountains!

Water! It's everywhere in Portland—flowing in the city's rivers and streams, coming down from the sky as rain, and spouting out of its many public fountains. When temperatures rise, Portlanders like to cool down in the city's many water features.

Jamison Square Fountain

One of the best is Keller Fountain, which is meant to look like the waterfalls of the lower Columbia River!

Teachers Fountain

TEACHERS FOUNTAIN
Dedicated to all who educate and ins

Salmon Street Fountain

Peninsula Park Fountain

GETTING AROUND

PORTLAND

In Portland, people drive cars, jump on buses, and use their own two feet to get around—it's a great city for walking! But here are some other ways Portlanders move from Point A to Point B.

PORTLAND STREETCAR

Streetcars: These vehicles have been operating in Portland since the late 1800s and played a big role in the city's growth and development. The modern system opened in 2001 and serves the downtown area.

Trains: MAX (Metropolitan Area Express) light rail makes many stops in Portland itself and connects the city with several surrounding towns, as well as the Portland International Airport.

Rollin' on the River(s): Do you like traveling in style? If so, you can book a short cruise on the *Portland Spirit*, a 150-foot luxury yacht that carries sightseers on waterway voyages around town. Or, if you're in the area May through October, you might want to take an old-style ride on the Columbia Gorge Sternwheeler (right), a triple-deck replica of the vessels that churned up and down the river in days gone by.

E-Scooters: Small electric two-wheelers can be rented via an app for one-way trips. Going no faster than 15 miles per hour, the scooters are energy efficient, and also fun to ride. Save your noggin— wear a helmet!

TRAM IT!

How do you get from down by the river to up in the mountains . . . without using a car? Take a ride (and check out the amazing views) from the Portland Aerial Tram. A large metal car rides on strong cables from the South Waterfront District to the Oregon Health and Science campus.

Opened in 2007.

Used by healthcare commuters, patients, and tourists.

Each car can hold 78 passengers and an operator.

Operating speed is 22 miles per hour.

Ride lasts three minutes.

Travels 3,300 feet horizontally and 500 feet vertically.

IT'S OFFICIAL!

Like other cities, Portland chose its favorite stuff to formally recognize. Here are some of the city's "official" things:

OFFICIAL CITY SONG:
"Portlandia"
"Portlandia" is also the name of a famous statue that watches over the city above the entrance to downtown's Portland Building. The sculpted woman is based on the female figure of the city's seal.

OFFICIAL CITY FLOWER:
The rose *(of course!)*

OFFICIAL CITY FLAG:
The colors symbolize forests (green), the grain harvest and "gold" of commerce (yellow), and the two main rivers (blue). The white star stands for Portland itself.

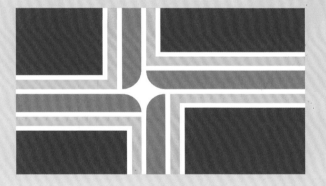

OFFICIAL OREGON STATE STUFF
Animal: Beaver
Bird: western meadowlark
Crustacean: Dungeness crab
Fish: Chinook salmon
Insect: Oregon swallowtail
Tree: Douglas fir
Flower: Oregon grape
Fruit: pear
Nut: hazelnut

Paul Bunyan: The legendary wood-cutting giant stands 31 feet high and weighs 3,700 pounds.

Art in Portland

Yes, that's one big lumberjack! His good friend, Babe the Blue Ox, must be grazing elsewhere. Paul Bunyan has towered over the North Portland neighborhood since 1959. The city offers many other places to view public art outside. And it's not just outside: See page 46 for details about great museums with indoor exhibits.

Outdoor Art

People in Portland love getting outside. Artists have created lots of remarkable creations for fresh-air seekers to check out.

Providence Park: Combine seeing the Portland Timber soccer team with art. This is *Facing the Crowd* by sculptor Michael Stutz.

People's Bike Library of Portland: Also called *The Pile*, it's basically a large stack of bikes on a pillar.

Allow Me: This life-sized guy is also known as *Umbrella Man*. You can probably guess why!

Museums— Go See 'Em!

In Portland, you can find a museum for almost any interest! Here are some you might like to visit:

Portland Art Museum (PAM): The museum has more than 50,000 objects in its collection! PAM displays art from ancient times to today, including many pieces made by the native peoples of North America.

Pittock Mansion: Built in 1914, this grand house once belonged to a rich and powerful family, the Pittocks. Today it belongs to the public. The mansion tells the story of how Portland went from a stump-filled pioneer town to a big modern city.

The Portland Institute for Contemporary Art (PICA): This museum not only showcases super-cool and modern paintings, sculptures, and installations, it also holds lots of artistic performances, like concerts and theatrical events.

Oregon Historical Society: Discover more about the people, places, and events that shaped Oregon, including the Portland Penny.

World Forestry Center: Not only do we all use wood products, we all breathe air made by trees! At this beautiful museum in Washington Park, you can find out about the world's forests and their importance to our lives.

Other Great Portland Museums

Museums are great for more than art, of course. Portland has something for just about everyone!

Oregon Rail Heritage Center: This railway museum houses awesome old steam locomotives. Imagine yourself taking a grand journey in the golden age of train travel . . . *All aboard!*

Kidd Toy Museum: Have you ever wondered what kids played with in the old days . . . like, in the *really* old days? Wonder no longer! This museum displays toys that were made from 1869 to 1939, including mechanical banks and vehicles.

Architectural Heritage Center: This is a great place to learn all about the history and design of Portland's buildings. You can also go on a walking tour and see some of the more famous ones for yourself!

Portland Puppet Museum: In a delightful old house from the 1870s, discover puppets and marionettes galore! You'll find puppet show stars like kings, queens, musicians, fairies, dragons, pandas, chickens, Dorothy and the Wizard of Oz gang, and many others.

Oregon Maritime Museum: When you board *The Portland*, you'll explore the last operating steam-powered sternwheel tug in the United States. Find out what life on the river was like in years gone by.

See the World in Portland

People have arrived in Portland from all over the globe. Their cultures and impacts on the area are celebrated at places like these.

Portland Chinatown Museum ➤ This museum educates visitors about the Chinese immigrant experience in the United States. It also tells the history of Portland's first truly multicultural neighborhood, Chinatown.

◄ Oregon Jewish Museum and Center for Holocaust Education: To help save and share the history of Jews and Judaism in Oregon, the museum exhibits artifacts and offers educational and cultural programs.

Nordic Northwest ➤ People from Denmark, Iceland, Finland, Norway, and Sweden have had a big influence on the Pacific Northwest. This facility celebrates their contributions. At the café, try *aebleskivers*—fluffy Danish pancake balls served with lemon curd, lingonberry jam, and maple syrup. Yum!

◄ Portland Japanese Garden: Take a trip to Japan by entering this peaceful paradise. It's not only a gorgeous garden, it's a cultural center where visitors can learn about traditional Japanese arts.

The Hellenic-American Cultural Center & Museum (HACCM): The art and experiences of Greek people in Portland are celebrated here.

Performing Arts

Portland offers almost any kind of live performance you'd care to attend. Here are some of the best-known and most popular:

Get an earful of amazing sound at the **Portland Opera**. These super-talented performers can really belt out a song!

Dancers! Check out the beauty and grace of the **Oregon Ballet Theatre** at the **Portland Center for the Performing Arts.**

In addition to traditional symphonies, the **Oregon Symphony** does performances of classical, pops, jazz, holiday, rock, and kids' orchestra music.

Every 4th of July weekend the **Waterfront Blues Festival** draws fantastic musicians, devoted fans, and lots of boaters who drop anchor near the show to listen in!

See all kinds of wonderful plays and musicals in great venues like **Portland Center Stage at the Armory, Artists Repertory Theatre, Northwest Children's Theater,** and **Oregon Children's Theatre.**

How to Talk Portland

Portlanders have their own way of saying things. Here's what you need to know to talk like the locals:

"RUNNING OVER TO FREDDY'S"

Going grocery shopping at a store in the large Fred Meyer chain.

MAX

is not a person. It's the name of the light rail line—the Metropolitan Area Express.

COUCH STREET

Rhyme it with *smooch*, not with *grouch*.

PDX

could refer to either the Portland International Airport or the city itself.

Sunbreaks

Blasts of sunshine that cut through the clouds.

Spendy

That just means something is expensive.

PORTLAND: It's Weird!

KEEP PORT

Airport Carpet

Portlanders love their airport, and they also love their airport's carpet. A lot. The unusual, teal-colored floor covering is a favorite backdrop for travelers' pictures—of their feet. You can even buy socks that match the giant rug's pattern. Wear them when you photograph your own tootsies. Why? Well . . . why not?!

Portlandia

From 2011-2018, the comedic TV show *Portlandia* spoofed the city's oddball ways. And that was just fine with Portlanders. They'd rather be strange than boring!

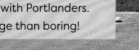

National Hat Museum

Located in a charming old house, this place contains the largest collection of hats on display in the United States. See 2,000 head-toppers of all kinds!

AND WEIRD

The Freakybuttrue Peculiarium and Museum

Have you ever wanted to see a bathtub full of guts or a parlor that serves ice cream—with insects in it? How about a massive, hairy Bigfoot? (It's not a real-life Sasquatch . . . or is it?!) Here you'll find these and many more oddities!

Naked Bike Ride

On a designated evening in June, thousands of Portlanders jump on their bikes wearing very little clothing or no clothing at all. They cruise around town in a big, happy, bare-skinned, party-on-the-go. And nobody gets their pants stuck in their bike chain!

Colorful Characters

Portland is known for its interesting folks about town. For example, there's a guy who wears a Darth Vader mask . . . while riding a unicycle . . . while playing the bagpipes . . . which sometimes have flames shooting out. That's the Unipiper!

Beverly Cleary

1916–2021

Maybe you've read some of the 30 books by beloved children's book writer Cleary (who, by the way, lived to be 104!). She was one of the first authors to write about regular kids doing regular stuff. Many of her books are set in her own Portland childhood neighborhood, Grant Park. In the park itself stand statues of her famous characters Ramona (the pest), Henry Huggins, and dog Ribsy.

Matt Groening

Born 1954

His last name rhymes with "raining." And that's fitting, because he grew up in Portland! Then he went on to create one of the funniest, most popular, and longest-running shows in TV history: the animated show called *The Simpsons*. Groening liked to give characters last names that are Portland streets. Hello, Ned Flanders, Mayor Quimby, Reverend Lovejoy, Millhouse Van Houten, and Sideshow Bob Terwilliger!

What People Do
IN PORTLAND

About 665,000 people live in the city of Portland. If you count everyone in the surrounding towns, the area's population jumps to about 2.5 million. Here are some of the most common ways they make a living.

major athletic shoe and sportswear companies like Nike and Columbia are headquartered in the area. Footwear giant Adidas chose Portland for its North American headquarters. These businesses employ thousands of people in all sorts of jobs.

So many high-tech companies are based in the Portland area that it got yet another nickname: The Silicon Forest. Lots of smart people work to keep these computer and electronics businesses going and growing.

The timber industry has always been huge in Portland—after all, the place started as "Stumptown." Local companies rely on large groups of employees to cut the trees, turn them into boards and wood products . . . and then plant more trees.

With several big hospital and medical facilities (including the Oregon Health & Science University complex), the Portland area has plenty of healthcare jobs to go around.

Lots of specialized things are made in the Portland area, like high-tech electronics and complex metal products, as well as food and drinks like craft beer, wine, cheese, and organic products. Manufacturers rely on their employees to run their factories, breweries, and offices.

The Port of Portland plays an important role in moving products and materials in and out of the Northwest. Many people work hard to make sure all that shipping runs smoothly.

Eat the Portland Way

Portlanders take their food very seriously! Their restaurants turn fresh, local ingredients into exciting new dishes. Their food carts (62-63) offer almost anything imaginable that's good to eat. And their farmers markets sell plenty of just-picked produce that they cook up at home.

Fish Food As residents of a river city that's not far from the ocean, Portlanders love fish—especially salmon! They cook and serve it many ways: grilled, smoked, baked, fried, raw, on skewers, in tacos, in salads—you name it! But salmon is not the only fish they eat. Halibut, from cold Pacific waters, is also a favorite. So are steelhead trout from Northwest rivers. Dungeness crab, oysters, and razor and bay clams from the Oregon coast also make it onto their dinner plates.

Veggie Heaven Portland is often ranked as the best city in the United States to be a vegetarian or vegan. If you like plant-based foods, you will find plenty of tasty things to eat!

Berry Good! Have you ever heard of marionberries? These sweet-but-tangy fruits were developed in Marion County, Oregon and are a Portland summertime treat. One of the very best ways to eat them is in a slice of pie . . . with a scoop of vanilla ice cream on top!

FAST FACT
Halibut can get huge—really, really huge. Sometimes they hit 500 pounds. That's a lot of fish sticks!

Speaking of Ice Cream . . . You've likely eaten Tillamook products, like cheese, butter, yogurt, and, yes, ice cream. The milk in those foods comes from dairies not far from Portland.

Nuts for Hazelnuts
The Willamette Valley (Portland sits at the top of it!) has the ideal climate for growing these tasty nuts. In fact, more than 99 percent of the hazelnuts grown in the United States come from Oregon trees!

Fungus Among Us
Mushrooms grow well in the damp forests of Oregon. Some Portlanders love to hunt for favorites like morels, golden chanterelles, and king boletes. But leave the picking to the experts—lots of mushrooms are poisonous to eat!

FOOD CART FEVER

Most people like to drive to restaurants. Portlanders like their restaurants to drive to them.

In recent years Portland has become known for its huge food cart scene. The popularity of these mobile kitchens has exploded in the past decade. But some people think the craze really started in 1965, when a wheeled hot-dog stand opened downtown, near City Hall. Unlike many other places, Portland put out the welcome mat and made it fairly easy for anyone with an equipped truck and a knack for cooking to find a spot and open shop.

Today, parked-cart clusters known as pods can be found in almost every neighborhood. About 600 vehicles offer up a moveable feast of almost any kind of food imaginable, including regional dishes from all over the world, vegan and gluten-free fare, savory standards, spicy specialties, and sweet snacks. So, while it's always easy to find this type of famous "fast food" in Portland, it's not always easy to decide what to order!

FAST FACT
A group of food carts parked together is called a pod. Portland has more than 20 pods!

Go, Portland Sports!

Portland is home to some awesome pro sports teams. Go, team, go!

Damian Lillard

PORTLAND TRAIL BLAZERS

Joined the National Basketball Association in 1970.

• Just call 'em "the Blazers"! The team has gone to the NBA Finals three times and won the NBA championship in 1977.

• The Blazers sold out 814 consecutive home games, from 1977 through 1995. That's the longest streak in NBA history.

Big Names: Clyde Drexler, Damian Lillard, Bill Walton, Terry Porter, Arvydas Sabonis

Home: Moda Center

Portland got one of its nicknames when the play-by-play announcer Bill Schonely yelled out "Rip City, baby!" after a Blazers guard made a long-distance shot in a 1971 game against the Los Angeles Lakers.

Diego Chara

PORTLAND TIMBERS

Joined Major League Soccer in 2009.

• In 2015 the Timbers won the championship game, the MLS Cup.

• Famous for selling out every single home game in team history. Also famous for the Timbers Army, a group of very loud and enthusiastic fans!

Big Names: Diego Valeri, Diego Chara, Darlington Nagbe, Sebastian Blanco, Fanendo Adi

Home: Providence Park

PORTLAND THORNS

Joined the National Women's Soccer League in 2012.

• In 2013 the Thorns won the first NWSL championship. They won it again in 2017!

• In a 2019 game, the team set a NWSL attendance record—of more than 25,000 fans—when it sold out its stadium.

Big names: Tobin Heath, Christine Sinclair, Alex Morgan, Lindsey Horan, Amandine Henry

Home: Providence Park

FAST FACT

In 1903, the Portland Beavers minor league baseball team began. The city supported the Beavers for more than 100 years, until the team moved to another city in 2010. Many people hope professional baseball will return to Portland soon!

PORTLAND WINTERHAWKS

Canadian Hockey League (CHL)

• Won the Ed Chynoweth Cup three times and the Memorial Cup twice.

• The team has been highly successful at producing National Hockey League (NHL) players.

Big Names: Dennis Holland, Randy Heath, Ray Podloski, Ty Rattie, Layne Roland

Home: Moda Center and Veterans Memorial Coliseum

Other Sports!

Portlanders love to be outdoors and they love staying active. Here are some other ways they have fun and get exercise:

In the home of Nike world headquarters and Adidas' North American operations, it's not surprising that **running** is a major sport. Big yearly races include the Portland Marathon and the Hood to Coast—the world's largest running relay race. Starting high up Mount Hood, 12,000 participants run 200 miles (in shifts) . . . all the way to the Pacific Ocean!

It's River City—so of course **river sports** are big! Portlanders enjoy kayaking, canoeing, paddle boarding, sailing, motor boating, windsurfing, and fishing. Every summer thousands of people jump onto and into rafts and innertubes and cruise down the Willamette in a slow-moving event known as the Big Float.

Portland's mild climate means players can **golf** 12 months a year. Sure, they sometimes get wet, but the rain keeps the greens, well . . . very green!

Cricket? Yes, cricket! Portland has many fans of this English sport. The Oregon Cricket League holds year-round matches.

Portlanders love to **snow ski**, **cross country ski**, and **snowboard** on nearby Mount Hood. Timberline is the only U.S. resort that offers skiing all year 'round!

Rock climbing is a popular activity in the area. Portland itself boasts several "crags," which are steep and rugged rocks that give climbers a good challenge.

COLLEGE TOWN

Portland is home to universities of many sizes and types. Maybe you'll attend college in the Rose City some day!

PORTLAND STATE UNIVERSITY

Founded 1946
Students: 27,000
Popular majors: business, social sciences, health professions
Fast Fact: PSU's campus sits on the city's South Park Blocks, a long greenspace in the heart of the city's cultural district.

UNIVERSITY OF PORTLAND

Founded 1901
Students: 4,200
Popular majors: health professions, business, engineering
Fast Fact: UP is a private Catholic university located on "the Bluff"—a cliff overlooking the Willamette River.

LEWIS & CLARK COLLEGE

Founded 1867
Students: 3,200
Popular majors: social sciences, biological and biomedical sciences, psychology
Fast Fact: The L&C campus is known as one of the most beautiful in the country.

REED COLLEGE

Founded 1908
Students: 1,400
Popular majors: economics, biology, linguistics and comparative literature
Fast Fact: Reed doesn't emphasize grades, and a large number of its graduates go on to earn graduate degrees.

WARNER PACIFIC UNIVERSITY

Founded 1937
Students: 1,500
Popular majors: education, accounting, human development and family studies
Fast Fact: WPU is a private Christian liberal arts university on the slope of Mount Tabor.

LOL!
Rose City Humor

Go ahead and laugh at Portland—its people won't mind! Here are some riddles to tickle your funny bone.

Why does Santa want to move to Portland?

Because he likes the rain, dear.

What is Portland's favorite card game?

Bridge.

Which Trail Blazers player can jump higher than a house?

All of them—houses can't jump.

What happened to the popularity of Portland's favorite flower?

It rose.

Why do some people think the east coast Portland is more important than the west coast Portland?

Because they consider it the Maine one.

What was Portland's first name?

I don't know. I'm stumped.

Why do Portlanders with pet hair allergies sneeze a lot?

Because the city has many firs.

What do Portlanders call a salmon that hits them in the face?

A sockeye.

What happens to Portlanders when they fall into the Willamette River?

They get wet.

It's Alive! Animals in Portland

Even though Portland is an urban area, it contains a surprising amount of wildlife. More than 300 kinds of mammals, birds, and fish live in or near its rivers, parks, woods, fields, yards, and gardens. Here are just some of the animals that call Portland home.

Western painted turtles

Columbian white-tailed deer

Woodpeckers

Pacific giant salamanders

Pacific tree frogs

Great horned owls

Swifts at Chapman Elementary

Every September evening, families pack picnics and gather at Chapman to catch the best show around. Several thousand Vaux's swifts swirl above the school's old chimney (thankfully, it's no longer used!). As dusk hits, the birds zoom headfirst down the brick shaft, one by one. The bird cloud finally clears when all the swifts are safe inside for the night. . . . and the crowd goes wild!

It's Alive! River Animals

Lots of animals live in or near Portland rivers. Take a hike along one of the city's many waterside paths and keep watch. Maybe you'll spot some of these amazing creatures!

Minks

Chinook salmon

Bald eagles

Rainbow trout

Ospreys

Great blue herons

Thank You, Beavers!

Beavers are famous for chewing and toppling trees. Surprisingly, these furry little lumberjacks don't hurt the environment— they help it! How? The busy critters stack logs in streams to create dams. The stopped water pools up. Voila: ponds! The beaver-made mini-lakes make great homes, not only for beavers, but for many other kinds of animals, and plants as well!

WE SAW IT AT THE ZOO

Siberian tiger

Have you been to the Oregon Zoo? If not, you *otter* go see the sea otters . . . and other wonderful animals!

The Oregon Zoo attracts 1.5 million visitors a year, making it the most popular tourist destination in the state! It all started back in 1888, when a seaman-turned-pharmacist named Richard Knight donated two bears to the city. Over the years, more and more animals were added to the Washington Park site. Today more than 1,800 furry, feathery, and scaly critters live there. Walk the zoo path to see playful penguins, gawky giraffes, mischievous monkeys, and many others. Or ride the train—and be sure to wave to the animals as you roll by.

Rainbow lorikeet

ZOOLIN

Excellence for Elephants

Packy was a famous Asian elephant born at the Oregon Zoo in 1962. He inspired people to learn how to better care for captive elephants. In 2015 the zoo opened a large enclosure with things that these smart, social animals would encounter in the wild, like mud wallows and a water hole. There's also a big heated indoor shelter with ground that's easy on those big elephant feet!

Lion cub

Sea otter

AFRICA SAVANNA

Off to Africa!

When the warm, moist air of the Africa Rainforest exhibit hits your face, you'll think you've wandered into a real jungle! Bats and tropical birds perch high in the trees while slender-snouted crocodiles, Nile monitor lizards, and lungfish lounge in waters below. And what's that big bundle of quills waddling by? Why, it's none other than an African crested porcupine!

Park Paradise!

Portland loves its parks! Here are just some of the city's favorites:

Mill Ends Park: This one made it into the *Guinness Book of World Records* for being the tiniest park on the planet. At just 452 square inches, there's not much to this park except a tree rising from a small planter.

Forest Park: From smallest . . . to biggest. This is the largest urban forest in the country. Here you can stroll on 80 miles of trails through 5,200 woodsy acres.

Director Park: A cool urban space, this park holds lots of free events, like concerts, art activities, chess games, plays, and more.

Mount Tabor

Would you like to play basketball in a volcano crater? You can when you come to this park. (Don't worry—the volcano is no longer active!) You'll

find a playground, forest walking paths, and incredible 360-degree views that let you see for miles and miles!

Laurelhurst Park: This charming park has something for everyone: a duck pond, playgrounds, picnic areas, dog run, basketball courts, volleyball courts, tennis courts, soccer fields—and even horseshoe pits!

Willamette Park: This is a great place to get near the river. It also has a dock and ramp to make it easy for boaters and kayakers to get on the river.

Council Crest: At 1,073 feet above sea level, this is the highest point in Portland. If you come on a clear day, you'll probably be able to spot nearby mountains—Mt. Hood, Mt. St. Helens, and Mt. Adams. You might even get a glimpse of Mt. Rainier, far to the north!

Spooky Sights

Ghosts! Many people think they're just a part of our imaginations, but others believe in them. Some even tell tales of their creepy sightings of misty, wispy beings. The following Portland places *just might* be haunted:

Is that a phantom in your popcorn? Years ago, a maintenance man died backstage at the famous old **Bagdad Theatre**. People claim they've heard his ghost whispering. Some even say they've seen it floating in front of the movie screen. Hey, down in front!

Cream, sugar, or spirits? **Rimsky-Korsakoffee** is a famous Portland coffee cafe located in a grand old house built in 1902. Some workers and customers say the place is haunted by two Russian writers who occasionally play classical music!

Would you like a poltergeist with that pepperoni pizza? Nina was a woman who worked at the Merchant Hotel more than 100 years ago. According to legend, bad guys killed her by pushing her down an elevator shaft. When the hotel became **Old Town Pizza** in the 1970s, Nina's gowned ghost stayed on. Some say they've smelled her perfume or heard her voice!

Are there souls in the saloon? **The White Eagle Saloon** says it shelters several ghostly people, including a young woman named Rose, a bartender named Sam, and some of the Shanghai Tunnels' kidnapping victims.

Is that a spook among the books? Workers at the **North Portland Library** report they've seen a shadowy male figure and heard his steps following them down the aisles.

Favorite Buildings

Portland has always had some very cool buildings. Old or new, they bring pizzazz to the city!

Pioneer Courthouse, 1869: The oldest federal government building in the Pacific Northwest.

Weinhard Brewery, 1862: An historic ale-making complex that still makes beer within its red-brick buildings.

Portland City Hall , 1895: A four-story Italian Renaissance-style building that houses city government and takes up an entire block.

Union Station, 1896: Known for its clock tower, Italian marble interior walls and floors, and the neon sign that urges travelers to "Go By Train."

Multnomah County Library, 1913: A gorgeous and ornate temple to books that's ranked as the busiest library in the entire country.

US Bancorp Tower, 1983: A 42-story skyscraper nicknamed "Big Pink" for its rosy color.

Oregon Convention Center, 1989: A well-known and distinctive part of the Portland skyline, with twin towers that bring bridge spires to mind.

Fair-Haired Dumbbell, 2017: An office building covered in colorful designs whose skybridges vaguely resemble the handle of, yes, a dumbbell.

Not Far Away

From Portland, you can drive to the ocean and play in the sand, and then drive up a mountain and play in the snow—on the same day! That's because the city is close to a lot of great attractions. Here are some of the most popular nearby destinations.

We went west! And look what we saw!

Wow! That's beautiful! Where is that?

It's **Cannon Beach**, right on the Pacific Ocean. It was only about 90 minutes from PDX!

What did you find on the beach?!

There are great tidepools, and this huge **Haystack Rock**. We even rented bikes and rode on the sand!

Was there more than just beachcombing?

Yes! North of Cannon Beach is a town called **Seaside**. We had a blast there.

There's an aquarium, a carousel, bumper cars, and even more cool beaches.

Looks like we need to get out of town and head to the beach!

FAST FACT
Mount Hood is 11,250 feet tall!

We just got back from **Mount Hood**. It was awesome.

That's the one we can see from town, right?

Well, when the weather is right!

Was there any snow?

You bet. It was spring and we had a snowball fight. We also got in some snowboarding.

Cool. I heard there was a camp there, too.

Yes, I'm trying to talk my parents into letting us go this year!

Did it take long to get to Mount Hood?

Barely over an hour! When we got there, look what we did!

Not Far Away

Wow! Where is that?

Multnomah Falls. It's only about 30 miles from Portland.

How tall is it?

More than 600 feet!

Where does the water go?

It all splashes into the Columbia River. The drive over here was gorgeous!

What else did you do out there?

After the Falls visit, we saw the **Bonneville Dam** and the fish ladder.

WHUT?

It's like the salmon ladder in Seattle. It lets fish get back upstream past the dam.

Cool!

Then we drove on the Froot Loop—not the cereal, but a road past tons of fruit trees!

What do you call the biggest airplane ever?

I don't know—what?

The **Spruce Goose!**

I saw it at the **Evergreen Aviation and Space Museum.**

It's huge! How did it fly?

Not very well! It only took off once, back in 1947.

Still pretty cool. What else did you do there?

They have an awesome **Wings & Waves Waterpark.**

Splash!

Then it was off to **Crater Lake.** It was a volcano long ago and has filled with water.

Sister Cities Around the World

Would you like having lots and lots of sisters? Portland sure does! Under the Sister Cities program, Bridgetown is officially connected with nine urban areas around the world. Sisters Cities pair up so that their citizens can get to know each other, learn about one another's cultures, and work together on projects. Many people think forming global friendships is a fine way to help keep the peace. Portland got its first Sister City in 1959, when it connected with Sapporo, Japan. Since then, it's joined up with eight more cities. These are the places Portland considers "family."

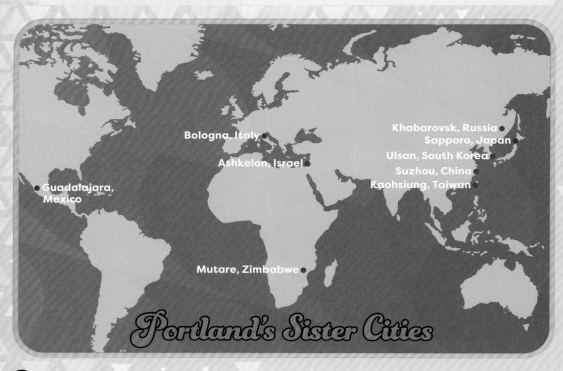

Bologna, Italy

Ashkelon, Israel

Khabarovsk, Russia
Sapporo, Japan
Ulsan, South Korea
Suzhou, China
Kaohsiung, Taiwan

Guadalajara, Mexico

Mutare, Zimbabwe

Portland's Sister Cities

Sister Cities in Action

Here are some ways Portland and its Sister Cities make cultural connections and help each other out:

Sapporo: Portland's longest Sister City relationship started in 1959. The cities have enjoyed many business and artistic opportunities over more than six decades. In 1988, Sapporo gifted Portland a "Peace Bell." It stands at the Oregon Convention Center plaza.

Bologna: During summer, teens from Bologna visit Portland and stay with local families. The next summer, the Portland teens from the host family travel to Bologna and stay with their former guests' families. Many lasting friendships have been formed this way!

Suzhou: Portlanders helped develop a sewage system for the 2,500-year-old Chinese city. And artists and craftspeople from Suzhou gave Portland a wonderful and enduring gift when they built the classical Lan Su Chinese Garden in Old Town!

Guadalajara: The cities have worked together on many projects, including firefighter training programs, cooking and food events, support for a Guadalajara school for autistic children, and a new rose garden for "The Rose City" of Mexico!

Books

Flynn, Brendan. *Portland Trail Blazers: All-Time Greats.* Press Box Books, 2020.

Gorton, Wendy. *50 Hikes with Kids: Oregon and Washington.* Timber Press, 2018.

Reynolds, Jennifer. *Oregon: The Coloring Book.* WestWinds Press, 2017.

Skewes, John. *Portland ABC.* Bigfoot Press, 2014.

Web Sites

travelportland.com/attractions/portland-rose-garden
See more beautiful pictures of roses.

omsi.edu
Amazing plants, cool machines, hands-on exhibits, and more: Check out the Oregon Museum of Science and Industry (OMSI)

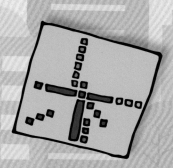

ohs.org
Find more about how Portland and the state of Oregon began.

powells.com/locations/powells-city-of-books
You're reading a book right now; this great store more!

oregonzoo.org
Can't see the animals in person? Meet lots of them on this web site of the Oregon Zoo.

worldforestry.org
The World Forestry Center site gives you a preview of the cool stuff to learn at this unique place.

Photo Credits and Thanks

Photos from Dreamstime, Shutterstock, or Wikimedia unless otherwise noted. Portland Art Museum: 15 top. Newscom: 64 top.

Artwork: Maps (6-7): Jessica Nevins.

Cultural Content Consultant: Jennifer E. Ellwood.

Thanks to our pal Nancy Ellwood and the fine folks at Arcadia!

Thanks for Visiting

Come Back Soon!